Jonathan's Book of Abstract Designs for Coloring

By Jonathan Jay Brandstater

For Lisa

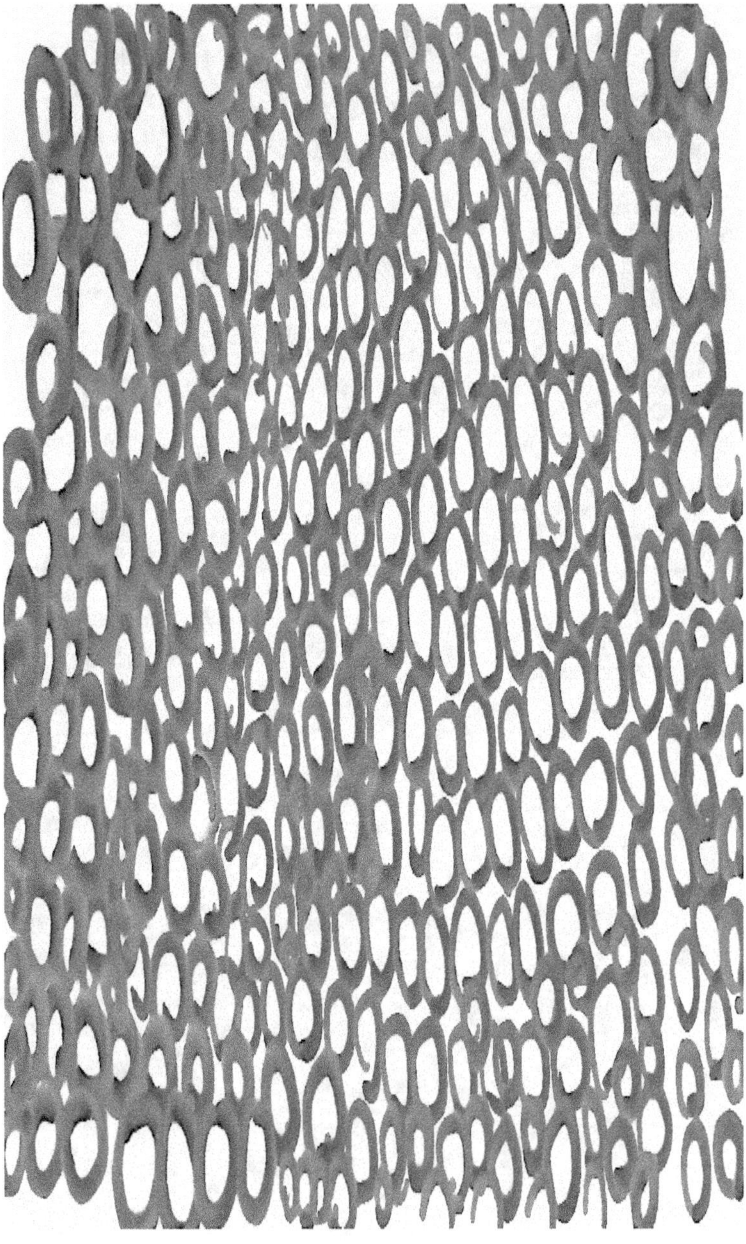

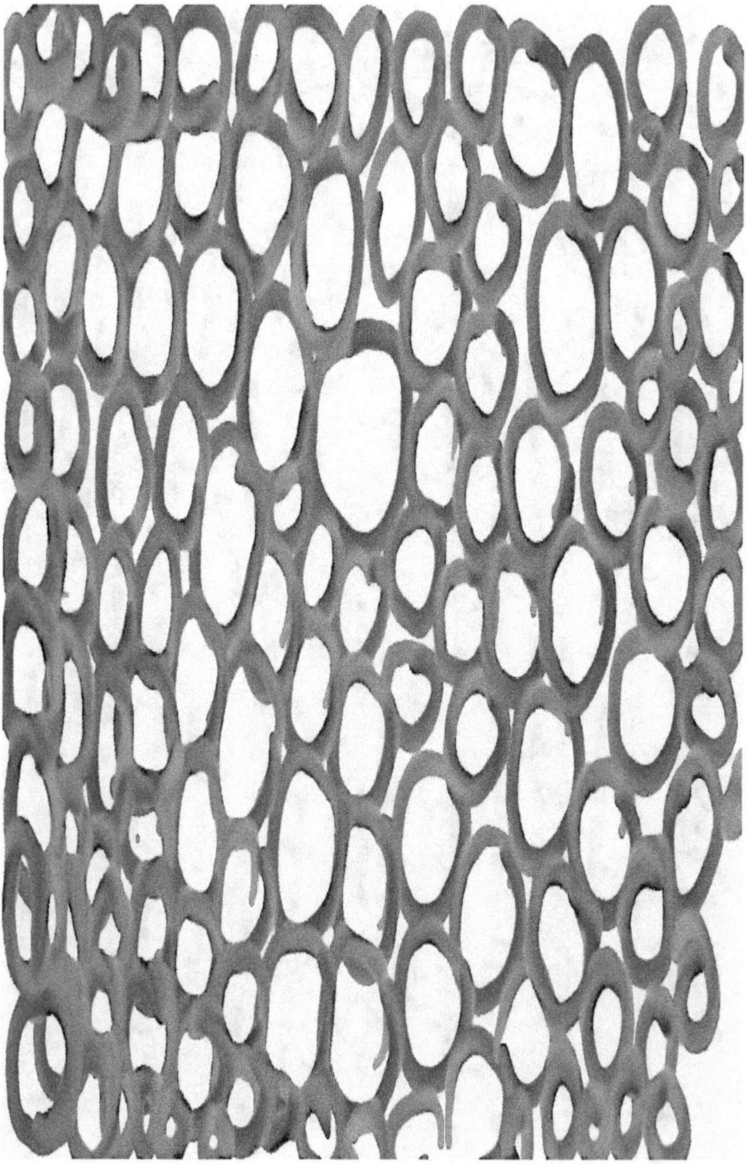

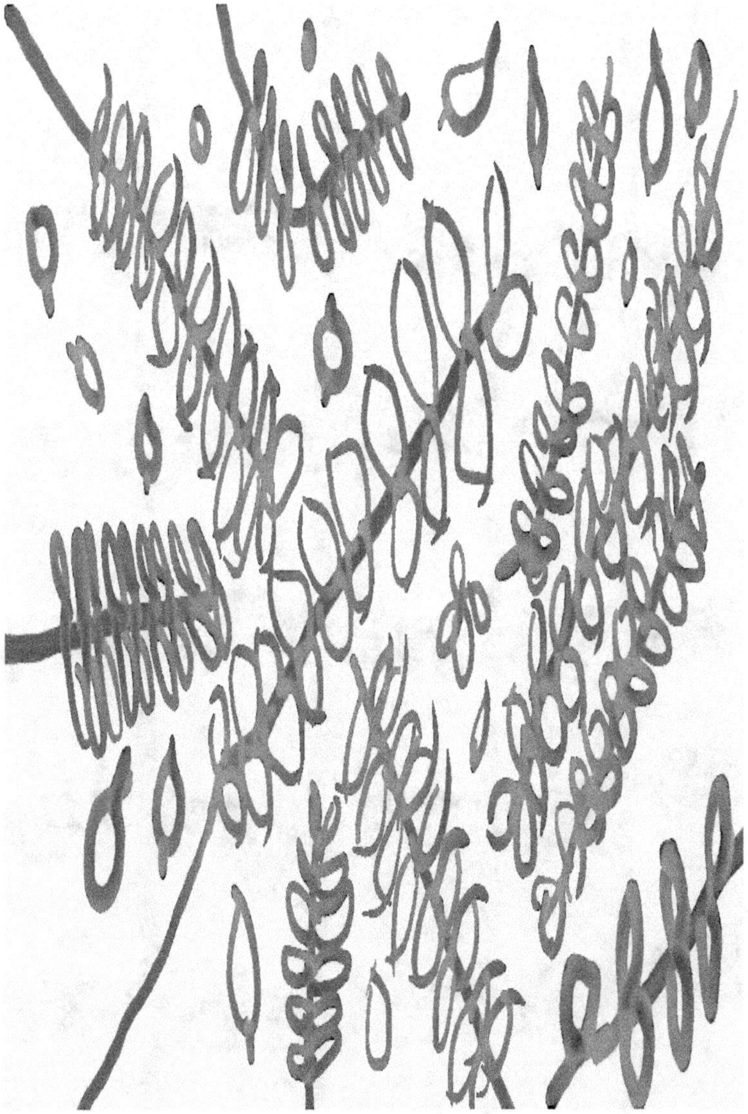

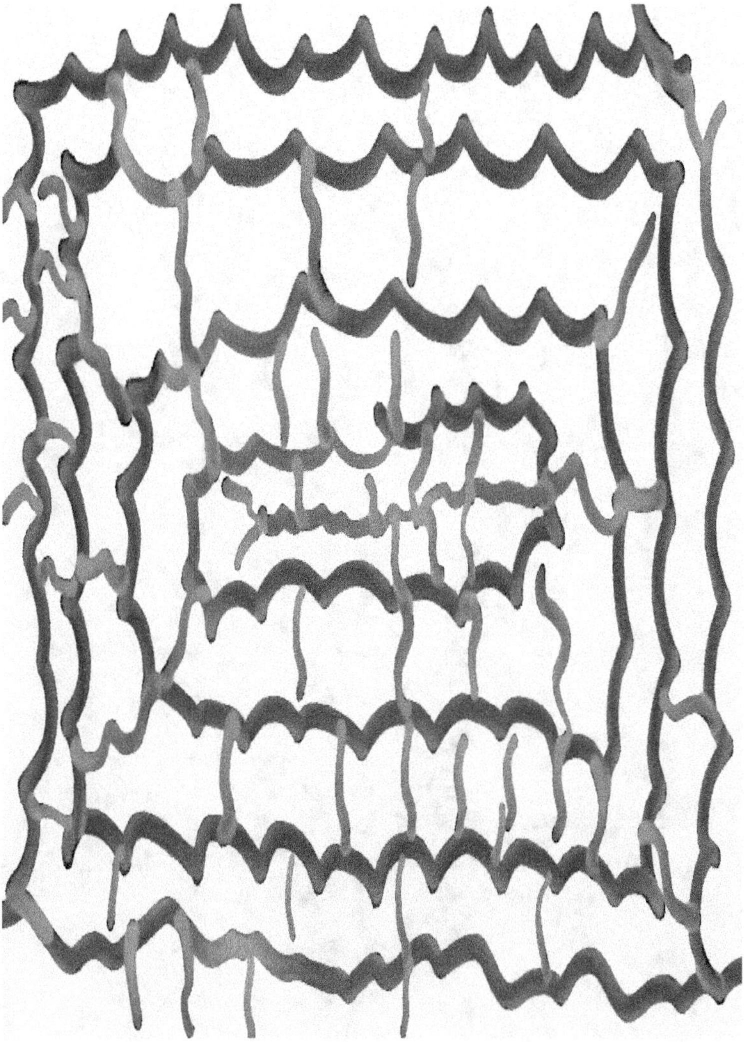

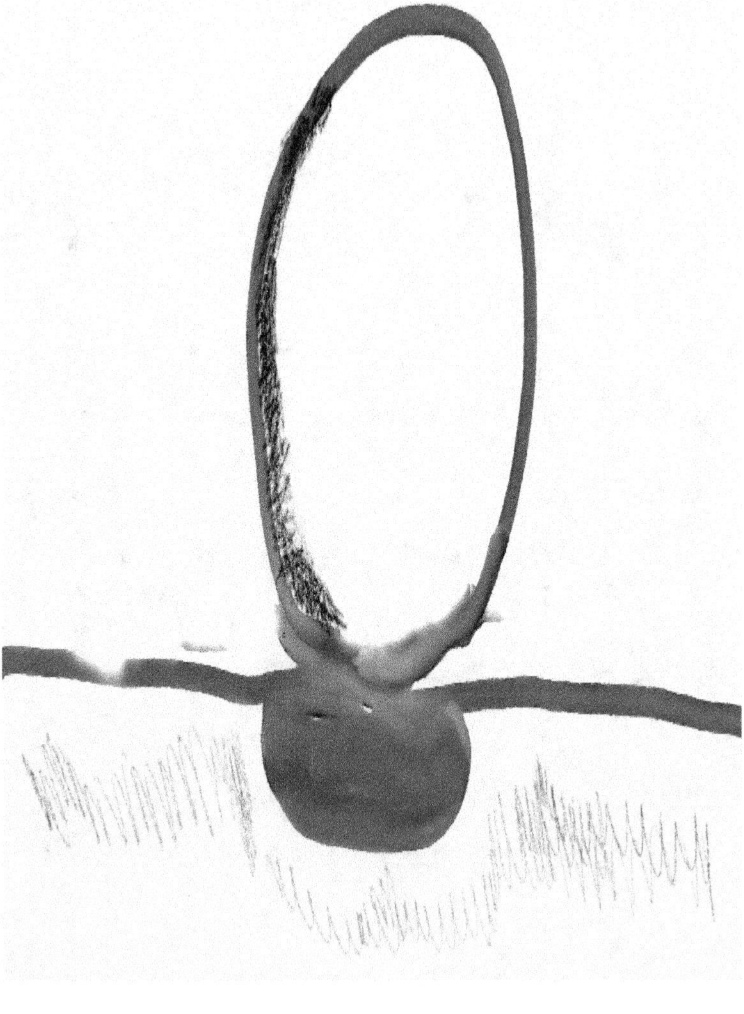

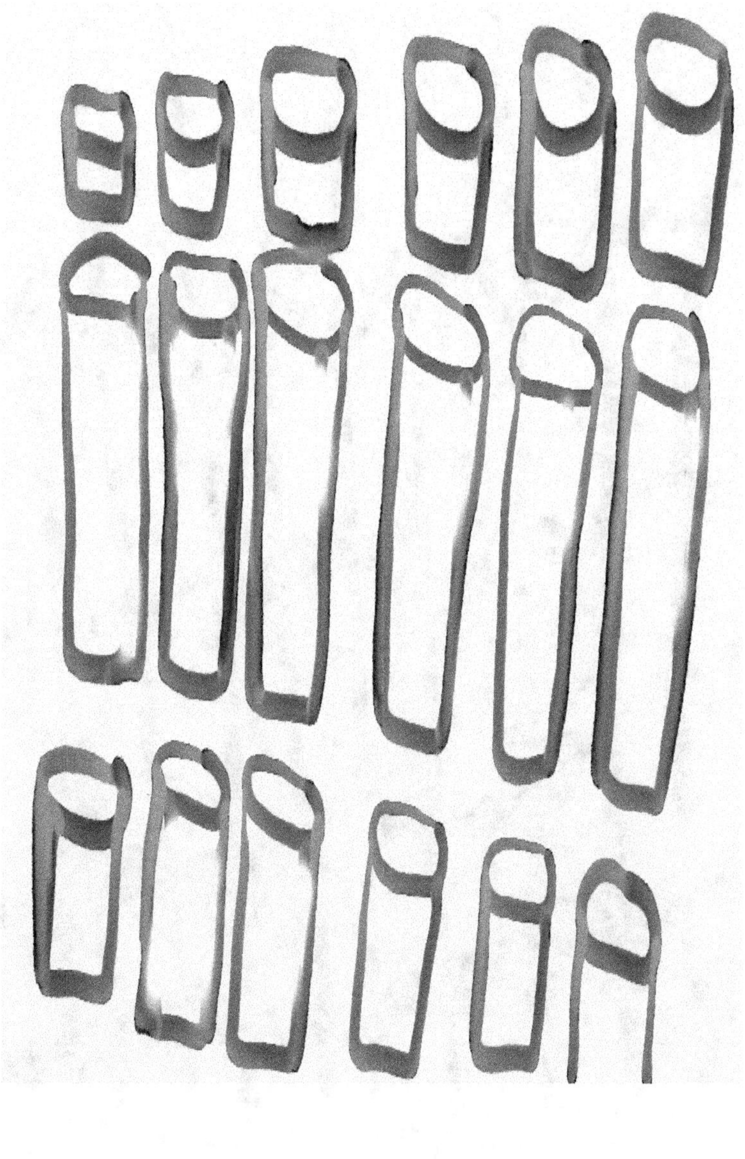

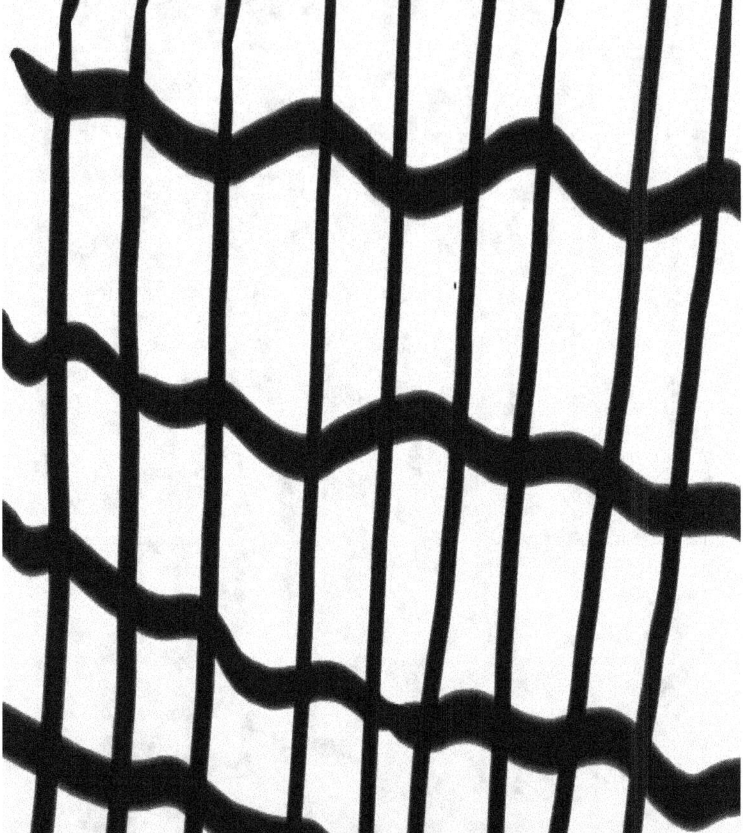

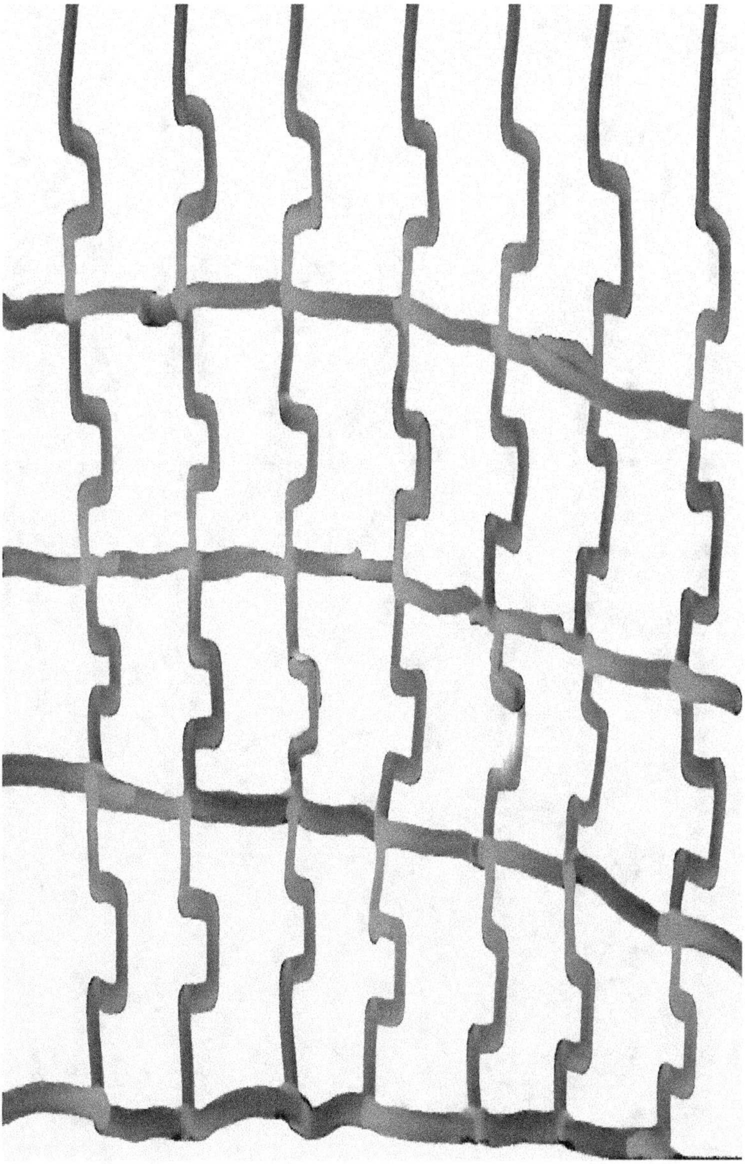

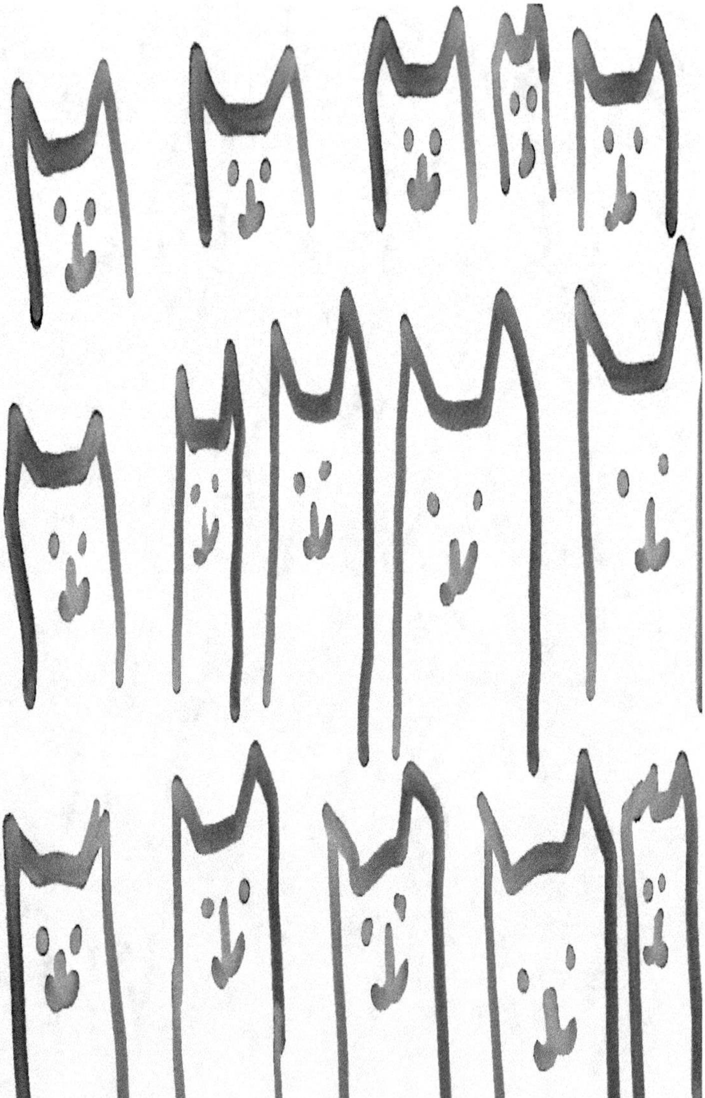

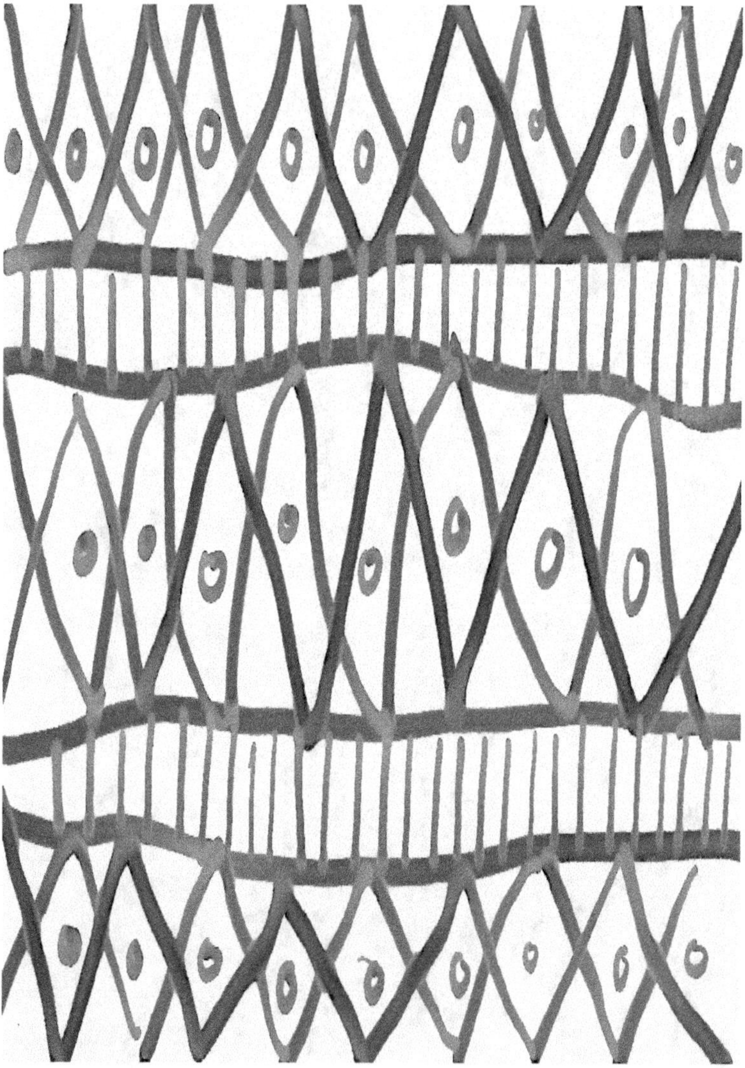

www.ingramcontent.com/pod-product-compliance
Lightning Source LLC
Chambersburg PA
CBHW071309280526
45788CB00004B/1866
9781543036541